What You Design?

by Debbie Allen

Glenview, Illinois
Boston, Massachusetts
Chandler, Arizona
Upper Saddle River, New Jersey

Picture Credits
Every effort has been made to secure permission and provide appropriate credit for photographic material.
The publisher deeply regrets any omission and pledges to correct errors called to its attention in subsequent editions.

Unless otherwise acknowledged, all photographs are the property of Pearson Education, Inc.

Photo locators denoted as follows: Top (T), Center (C), Bottom (B), Left (L), Right (R), Background (Bkgd).

Opener: (C) Andy Crawford/©DK Images; 2 (B) ©Adam Gault/Getty Images; 4 (B) ©ZouZou/Shutterstock; 5 (TL) ©PeppPic/Shutterstock, (B) ©Rey Kamensky/Shutterstock, (TR) Shutterstock; 7 (B) ©David Young-Wolff/PhotoEdit, Inc.; 8 (B) Katy McDonnell/Thinkstock; 9 (B) ©Laty McDonnell/Getty Images; 10 (L) ©Ewa Walicka/Shutterstock, (R) ©STILLFX/Shutterstock; 11 (R) ©Ewa Walicka/Shutterstock, (L) ©Nikola Bilic/Shutterstock; 13 (B) ©Katrina Brown/Shutterstock; 14 (B) ©Flying Colours Ltd./Getty Images; 15 (B) Jupiterimages/Thinkstock.

FP1 (B) ©Katrina Brown/Shutterstock; FP3 (L, CL) ©Ewa Walicka/Shutterstock, (R) ©liza1979/Shutterstock, (CR) ©Nikola Bilic/Shutterstock, (CR, CL) Shutterstock.

ISBN-13: 978-0-328-64458-2
ISBN-10:   0-328-64458-7

7 8 9 10 V0FL 18 17 16 15

What You Already Know

Technology is using science to solve problems.

People use technology to share ideas.

People use technology for new ideas.

Technology keeps people safe.

People need to solve problems.

They design and make things.

They choose materials to use.

Some materials are natural.

Others are made by people.

What materials do you see?

Find a Problem

You draw and write on paper.

You might throw away some paper.

You drink milk from plastic bottles.

You might throw away the bottles.

People throw away many things.

You can recycle paper and plastic.

You can recycle glass and metal.

Recycling makes less trash.

How can you recycle some things you use in class?

This is a problem.

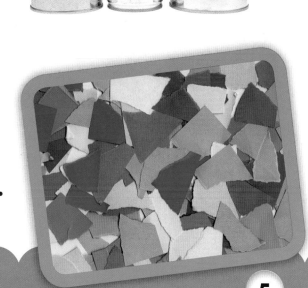

Some materials can be recycled.

Set a Goal

You can set a goal to solve the problem.

What can you do?

You can look in the trash for things to recycle.

That will be messy.

What do you see in this trash can that can be recycled?

Your goal is to make a classroom recycling center.

You will put some objects in recycling bins.

This will be easy to do.

It will not be messy.

A classroom recycling center will solve the problem.

Plan and Draw

Write a plan for the recycling center.

Tell how many bins you will need.

Tell how you will get materials.

Tell how you will put it together.

Tell if an adult will help.

Work with others to make a plan.

Draw a design for the recycling center.

Show how many bins you will use.

Show how the bins will look.

Label the parts of the design.

Label the materials you will use.

Draw your design.

Choose Materials

What materials will you use?

You need something to hold the objects.

You choose large boxes.

Choose the materials that will work best.

Bottles might be wet.

You choose garbage bags to put inside the boxes.

They will keep the boxes dry.

The garbage bags might slip.

You choose tape to keep them in place.

Make and Test

Make the recycling center.

Put a garbage bag inside a box.

Tape the top of the bag to the box.

Decide what the box will hold.

Choose paper or plastic or metal.

Label the box.

Make two more boxes.

plastic

Put the recycling center in your classroom.

Ask everyone to use it.

Check it at the end of the first day.

Look at the objects in the boxes.

Look at the objects in the trash can.

Check them each day for a week.

These materials can be recycled.

Record and Share

Write how your solution worked.

Did people recycle the right objects?

Can you make your design better?

You can paste pictures on each box.

They will show what goes in each bin.

Can you make your plan better?

Talk with others about your design.

Tell if your design solved the problem.

You can use your design again.

You can make a recycling center at home.

Families can recycle too.

Glossary

recycle   to treat something
so that it can be
used again

recycling center   place where objects
are recycled